How To Play Electric Guitar

Your Step-By-Step Guide To Playing The Electric Guitar

HowExpert

Copyright HowExpert™
www.HowExpert.com

For more tips related to this topic, visit www.HowExpert.com/guitar.

Recommended Resources

www.HowExpert.com – Quick 'How To' Guides on Unique Topics by Everyday Experts.

www.HowExpert.com/writers - Write About Your #1 Passion/Knowledge/Experience.

www.HowExpert.com/membership - Learn a New 'How To' Topic About Practically Everything Every Week.

www.HowExpert.com/jobs - Check Out HowExpert Jobs.

COPYRIGHT, LEGAL NOTICE AND DISCLAIMER:

COPYRIGHT © BY HOWEXPERT™. ALL RIGHTS RESERVED WORLDWIDE. NO PART OF THIS PUBLICATION MAY BE REPRODUCED IN ANY FORM OR BY ANY MEANS, INCLUDING SCANNING, PHOTOCOPYING, OR OTHERWISE WITHOUT PRIOR WRITTEN PERMISSION OF THE COPYRIGHT HOLDER.

DISCLAIMER AND TERMS OF USE: PLEASE NOTE THAT MUCH OF THIS PUBLICATION IS BASED ON PERSONAL EXPERIENCE AND ANECDOTAL EVIDENCE. ALTHOUGH THE AUTHOR AND PUBLISHER HAVE MADE EVERY REASONABLE ATTEMPT TO ACHIEVE COMPLETE ACCURACY OF THE CONTENT IN THIS GUIDE, THEY ASSUME NO RESPONSIBILITY FOR ERRORS OR OMISSIONS. ALSO, YOU SHOULD USE THIS INFORMATION AS YOU SEE FIT, AND AT YOUR OWN RISK. YOUR PARTICULAR SITUATION MAY NOT BE EXACTLY SUITED TO THE EXAMPLES ILLUSTRATED HERE; IN FACT, IT'S LIKELY THAT THEY WON'T BE THE SAME, AND YOU SHOULD ADJUST YOUR USE OF THE INFORMATION AND RECOMMENDATIONS ACCORDINGLY.

THE AUTHOR AND PUBLISHER DO NOT WARRANT THE PERFORMANCE, EFFECTIVENESS OR APPLICABILITY OF ANY SITES LISTED OR LINKED TO IN THIS BOOK. ALL LINKS ARE FOR INFORMATION PURPOSES ONLY AND ARE NOT WARRANTED FOR CONTENT, ACCURACY OR ANY OTHER IMPLIED OR EXPLICIT PURPOSE.

ANY TRADEMARKS, SERVICE MARKS, PRODUCT NAMES OR NAMED FEATURES ARE ASSUMED TO BE THE PROPERTY OF THEIR RESPECTIVE OWNERS, AND ARE USED ONLY FOR REFERENCE. THERE IS NO IMPLIED ENDORSEMENT IF WE USE ONE OF THESE TERMS.

NO PART OF THIS BOOK MAY BE REPRODUCED, STORED IN A RETRIEVAL SYSTEM, OR TRANSMITTED BY ANY OTHER MEANS: ELECTRONIC, MECHANICAL, PHOTOCOPYING, RECORDING, OR OTHERWISE, WITHOUT THE PRIOR WRITTEN PERMISSION OF THE AUTHOR.

ANY VIOLATION BY STEALING THIS BOOK OR DOWNLOADING OR SHARING IT ILLEGALLY WILL BE PROSECUTED BY LAWYERS TO THE FULLEST EXTENT. THIS PUBLICATION IS PROTECTED UNDER THE US COPYRIGHT ACT OF 1976 AND ALL OTHER APPLICABLE INTERNATIONAL, FEDERAL, STATE AND LOCAL LAWS AND ALL RIGHTS ARE RESERVED, INCLUDING RESALE RIGHTS: YOU ARE NOT ALLOWED TO GIVE OR SELL THIS GUIDE TO ANYONE ELSE.

THIS PUBLICATION IS DESIGNED TO PROVIDE ACCURATE AND AUTHORITATIVE INFORMATION WITH REGARD TO THE SUBJECT MATTER COVERED. IT IS SOLD WITH THE UNDERSTANDING THAT THE AUTHORS AND PUBLISHERS ARE NOT ENGAGED IN RENDERING LEGAL, FINANCIAL, OR OTHER PROFESSIONAL ADVICE. LAWS AND PRACTICES OFTEN VARY FROM STATE TO STATE AND IF LEGAL OR OTHER EXPERT ASSISTANCE IS REQUIRED, THE SERVICES OF A PROFESSIONAL SHOULD BE SOUGHT. THE AUTHORS AND PUBLISHER SPECIFICALLY DISCLAIM ANY LIABILITY THAT IS INCURRED FROM THE USE OR APPLICATION OF THE CONTENTS OF THIS BOOK.

COPYRIGHT BY HOWEXPERT™ – ALL RIGHTS RESERVED WORLDWIDE.

Table of Contents

Recommended Resources 2
Part 1 – Introduction 5
How the Electric Guitar Came To Be 6
Parts Of The Electric Guitar 8
   The Neck 8
   The Body 9
Part 2 – How To Get Ready To Play Electric Guitar 13
How To Select Your Guitar And Equipment 13
   Types of electric guitars 13
Effects And Other Peripherals 14
How To Set Up Your Electric Guitar 16
   Method 1 17
   Method 2 - Tuning With Harmonics 18
How To Set Up The Amplifier 20
Part 3 – How To Play Position & Basic Techniques 21
How To Sit Down And Hold The Guitar 22
Fretting 23
Picking using a plectrum 24
How To Use The Downstroke, The Upstroke And, The Economy Picking 25
The Two Ways To "Attack" The Strings: 26
Part 4 - Basic Chords and Scales 28
Notes and Scales 28
Demo: Star Spangled Banner 30
Chords 32
Part 5 - Conclusion 42
Electric Guitar Maintenance Tips 42
   How To Clean and Store Your Electric Guitar 42
   How To Change The Electric Guitar Strings 42
Hand And Body Care Tips 43
Practice Tips 43
VI. Chord Chart 45
Recommended Resources 51

Part 1 – Introduction

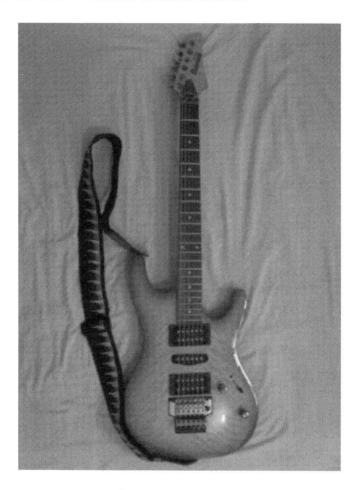

Electric bass (Ibanez)

Hi and welcome to "How to Play the Electric Guitar - A Beginner's Guide". In this e-book, we will tackle all the basic stuff you'll need to know to be able to start playing the electric guitar. Hopefully, at the end of this course you'll have the necessary skill, not only to play through a whole song but to pursue more advanced guitar studies as well.

Before we begin, I believe it is important for you to become really familiar with the electric guitar. Here are some fun and fascinating facts that will surely pique your interest in this very popular instrument.

How It Works

An electric guitar differs from an acoustic guitar mainly because it uses magnetic pickups and an amplifier to produce sound. Your pickups (shown later) can either be single coils or humbuckers, but both operate in pretty much the same way.

Since the strings are made out of metal, any vibration or oscillation it makes create changes in the magnetic field of the pickup. These changes are then converted into electrical signals which go into the amplifier and again get converted into sound waves.

How the Electric Guitar Came To Be

The idea of amplifying the sound of an instrument isn't new. Some patents from around 1910 show telephone transmitters being fitted inside violins and banjos so that the sound can be picked up and made louder. However, the idea of electric guitar was first introduced by Les Paul in the 1930's when he attached microphones to his guitars.

This was also the era when "big bands" were becoming popular. A regular guitar obviously couldn't compete with large brass sections so jazz guitarists started using hollow arch top acoustic guitars equipped with electromagnetic transducers.

These guitars sounded great for jazz, but players who wanted a more aggressive sound were limited by the feedback problem that accompanied hollow body guitars. The solid body electric guitar was then developed to overcome this limitation, the first instance of it being a cast aluminum electric steel guitar made by Rickenbacker nicknamed "The Frying Pan". Les Paul also created one from an Epiphone archtop guitar. Dubbed "the log guitar", it was constructed from a 4 x 4 solid wood post with homemade pickups and hardware.

With this guitar, Les Paul eventually went on to partner with the Gibson Corporation which gave birth to the Gibson Les Paul Model.

Parts Of The Electric Guitar

The Neck

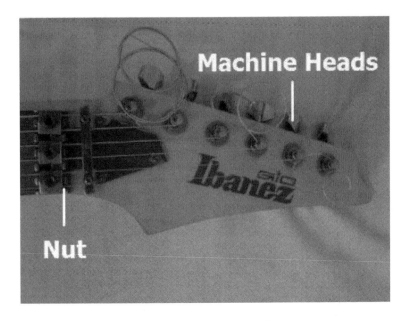

Electric Guitar Neck

1. **Machine heads** - This is where the other end of the string goes, and is used to change the tension of the string.
2. **Nut** - A thin strip that is typically made out of plastic, graphite or wood, it is used to hold the strings in place.
3. **Truss rod** - This is a metal rod within the neck of the guitar used to adjust neck relief. Neck relief is the distance between the frets and the strings. Do not attempt to adjust this yourself; you can break the neck of your guitar

if you do it incorrectly. Bring your guitar to a luthier instead if you want to have it adjusted.
4. **Frets** - These are the thin metal strips which divide the neck into pitch intervals.

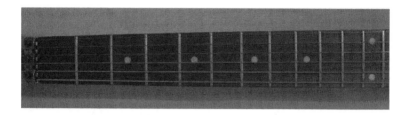

The Body

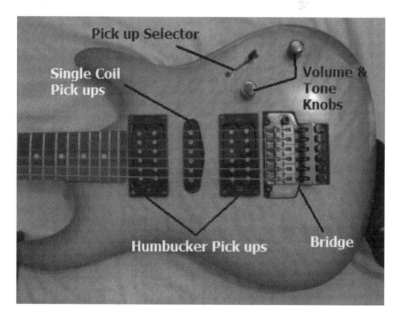

Electric Guitar Body

1. **Body** - Guitars bodies are either hollow or solid, with solid body electric guitars being the norm. Usually, the heavier and denser the wood of body, the better.
2. **Pickups** – Magnetic pickups literally pickup sounds from the vibration of the strings, then convert it to electrical signals to produce sounds that can be recorded.

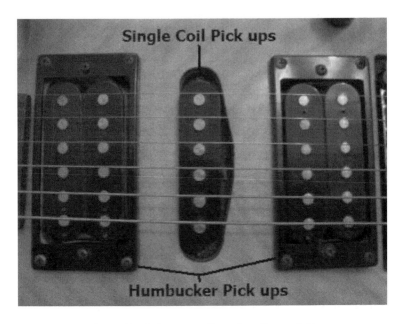

Single coil pick ups & humbucker pick ups

- **Jack socket** - This is where the end of jack or cable goes. Make sure you push the cable in until it locks.

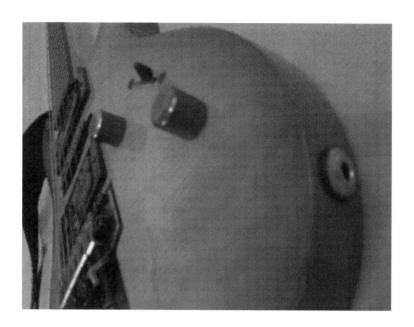

Jack Socket

- **Volume and Tone Knobs** - Use these to adjust the volume and the tone. Tone knobs often control the amount of treble or clarity on most guitars. Some guitars have more pickups and pickup positions that others, hence more tone knobs.

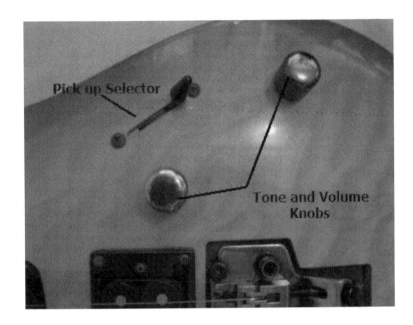

Pick up selector and tone & volume knobs

- **Bridge** - This is where the ball/bullet ends of the string go. There are several types of guitar bridges; the one on this guitar is a Floyd Rose Tremolo System. I would not recommend a guitar with a bridge like this to a beginner as it is very difficult to fix and tune. You'd do best to start with a guitar that has a FIXED BRIDGE.

Part 2 – How To Get Ready To Play Electric Guitar

How To Select Your Guitar And Equipment

Types of electric guitars

Electric guitars come in all sorts of shapes and sizes, and this is not mainly for aesthetic purposes. The type of guitar that you use will definitely influence your playing style, which is why I recommend a balanced and versatile guitar for beginners.

- **The Stratocaster** - If you are a beginner and you already own an electric guitar, chances are it will be a Fender Stratocaster, or something which closely resembles the "Strat". The Stratocaster is arguably the most popular type of electric guitar, and has practically come to symbolize the electric guitar the world over for a good reason: it is simple, yet very VERSATILE. If you don't have an electric guitar yet, I would recommend you get this one.
- **Amplifiers** - The amplifier plays a huge role in shaping your sound. Basically, there are 2 types of amplifiers: Tube amps and solid state amps. Tube or valve amplifiers use vacuum tubes to amplify the signal coming from your guitar while solid-state amplifiers use transistors and IC's. While guitarists in general praise tube amps because of their unique and

vintage sound, I would recommend that you get a decent 15 or 30 watt solid state amplifier instead since you'd probably be using this mostly for practice. Not getting too much into detail, a small solid state amp is a lot cheaper and requires less maintenance compared to a tube amp.

Effects And Other Peripherals

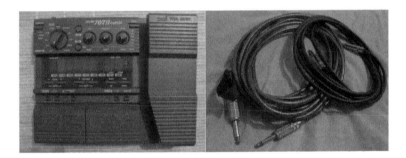

Effects and Cables

1. **Effects and pedals** - Effects processors, pedals and stomp boxes alter the signal from your guitar to the amplifier so you can have a broader palette of sound. The effects units available for the electric guitar can be mind boggling so we won't get too much into that, but for starters I would recommend that you start with an overdrive or distortion pedal, because you will need to practice playing with and without distortion.
2. **Cables** - Cables rarely differ in design and the tonal difference a regular cable makes is rarely

evident. While shielded and noiseless cables are ideal, these are often expensive and the benefits are often negligible in a regular session. You'll be better off buying reasonably priced cables for now, and in this case the brand name is often a good indicator of the quality. If in doubt, you can always ask if you can try them out on the spot, and you can also check the quality of soldering on the end plugs.

Strap and Pick

1. **Strap** - It can be easy to overlook the importance of the guitar strap, but this is something you should really invest in. An electric guitar can be very heavy, and your strap should be able to help you support this load comfortably so that the weight won't affect your playing. Get a good, sturdy strap, preferably made out of leather.
2. **Picks** - For starters, I would recommend that you get a Dunlop Tortex Standard pick. Thin picks are great for strumming while hard picks are better for fast picking. A sharper tip will give you more note definition and more

"attack" while a rounder tip will provide less resistance when picking.
3. **Strings** - Strings come in different gauges, which usually appear on the packaging like this:

.009 .011 .016 .024 .032 .042

String diameter is measured by thousandths of an inch, starting with the thin E, followed by the B, G, D, A and the thick E string. The thicker the gauge, the fuller and heavier the sound, although the gauge that you use should depend on what kind of sound you are trying to achieve. Thicker strings are also harder to fret and pick, which is why I recommend that you use a thinner gauge for now and just move to a thicker gauge if you prefer once you develop hand strength and dexterity.

4. **Tuner** - The tuner is another indispensable piece of equipment you should not be without. Most multi effects processors already have tuners built in, but if you don't have one, you can just buy a tuner separately. A tuner is an inexpensive piece of equipment that can be found at almost every music store.

How To Set Up Your Electric Guitar

Tuning the guitar - Always use your tuner to tune up your guitar. If you don't have a tuner, you can tune it by ear, but I certainly would not recommend this for a beginner! Your ears need to get used to the correct pitches and the only way to get in tune accurately is to use an electronic tuner. However, if there really is not tuner at hand, use the two following methods.

Method 1

- Start from the E6 string (the thickest string). It has to be in tuned exactly to E, otherwise all other strings will also be out of tune. Once in tune, fret it on the fifth fret (A), it should give you an A note. Then, lower the pitch of your A5 string. You have to do this so you can tune up until the pitch of your A5 string is in unison with the A note on your E6 string. Pick the A note on the E6 string and your A5 string in succession. Tune the A6 string up until its pitch is exactly the same as the A on the E6 string.
- Do the same on the A5 string: fret it on the fifth fret to get a D, tune down the D4 string then tune it up until both strings are in unison.
- Do the same on the D4 string: fret it on the fifth fret to get a G, tune down the G3 string then tune it up until both strings are in unison.
- On the G3 string, you will have to fret on the 4th fret instead of the 5th, since B is on the 4th. Again, tune down the B2 string then tune it up until both strings are in unison.
- Fret the B2 string on the fifth fret to get an E. Tune down the E1 string then tune it up until both strings are in unison, then pick the E6 and the E1 to check if they are in unison.

Method 2 - Tuning With Harmonics

This is a more accurate, although a bit trickier way of tuning your guitar. Instead of fretting your reference note, you will have to play it using "natural harmonics", which involves deftly touching the string at the correct position and then releasing it at just the right moment after picking.

A harmonic note is stripped of overtones, which is why the "timbre" of harmonic notes of the same pitch played on the different strings will sound almost exactly the same. This is what makes this method more accurate. To start, make sure that your E6 string is perfectly in tune. It will again act as your reference for tuning the A5 string.

The harmonic note you need to get on your E6 string is E. Gently place a finger on your E6 string, almost directly over the 5th fret wire. Release your fretting finger almost at the same time that you pick the string. The resulting note should sound a bit like a bell; it will be high pitched and even shrill if you have a bit of gain on. It should not sound muted or "round" or "full". This will take a bit of experimenting on your part, a bit of trial and error before you get used to the technique. You'll notice that a harmonic note rings out a bit longer than a fretted note.

Using the E harmonic note on your E6 string as reference, play a natural harmonic note on the A5 string by fretting gently over the 7th fret wire. Tune the A5 string up until it sounds EXACTLY the same as the harmonic E on the E6 string. Always tune UP to the desired note and not down, our ears are partial to higher pitches and run the risk of tuning slightly higher than your reference note if you're coming from a higher pitch.

The next two strings, the D4 and G3, can be tuned in the same manner: play the harmonic note on the 5th fret wire of the reference string, then play a harmonic note on the 7th fret wire of the string below it. Tune it up until both are in unison.

Now since the guitar is tuned in such a way that the B note happens to fall on the 4th fret of the G3, the tuning method we did earlier will not work. To tune your B2 string, play a harmonic note above the 7th fret wire of your E6 string. This should give you a correct B harmonic note. Play the open B2 string and tune up until it is in unison with the B harmonic note on the E6 string.

The E note will now be on the 5th fret of your B2 string. Play the harmonic note on the fifth fret wire of your B2 string, and then play the harmonic note on the 7th fret of your E1 string. Tune up until both are in unison.

- Since both methods will require you to have your E6 to be perfectly in tune, you will see that a tuner is still the BEST way to get your electric guitar in tune. It is a worthwhile investment since you'll still need to use it even if you progress to being an advanced player. It will also prove especially handy in situations where you won't be able to hear yourself tune, like gigs or if you don't have an amplifier to plug into.

How To Set Up The Amplifier

There are no "correct" settings for your amp. Just plug in your guitar and feel free to experiment. All you need to do is to get a sound that is pleasing to your ears. This is essential, because music is all about making sounds that you like to listen to.

Make sure the volume is just right; not too loud, not too soft. To avoid damaging your ears, you may need to use earphones. I like to use earphones when playing/practicing alone. This way, I can turn down the volume to block out external noise and at the same time listen closely to the quality of the notes I play without having to turn up the volume (and disturbing other people).

If your amplifier has an equalizer (Low, Mid, Treble), play around with it. This will definitely affect the way you play, and even your tone preference.

I personally prefer to raise the mid most of the time, and just play around with the lows and the highs depending on what I'm playing. I believe that the mid range is the natural range of the electric guitar, but it can be quite hard to play with a boosted mid range because it will also bring out your picking and muting mistakes.

Part 3 – How To Play Position & Basic Techniques

Since this is a beginner course, you will find that it can be very difficult to play standing up, which is why we'll need to focus more on playing while sitting down.

Some important things you'll need to keep in mind while playing:

- **Economy Of Motion** - This simply means that you'll need to keep all movements at a bare minimum in order to be efficient. For example, it is generally a good idea to lift your fretting finger just up to where it won't interfere with the vibration of the strings. Same goes for picking; don't let the tip of the pick wander off too far from the string. This is something you'll want to develop early on as this will enable you to play more difficult passages later on.
- **Playing Without Tension** - You'll be able to play in a more relaxed manner if you are efficient in your movement and vice versa. The only way to achieve this is to develop the muscles in your hand, arm and back. Being physically fit will also help. The rationale behind this is that muscles in good condition move better and last longer. While finger exercises will help, it may not be necessary since your fingers will be getting enough of that

during practice. On the other hand, arm and back exercises will definitely help.

By the way, your muscles need to be flexible as well, so don't forget to do stretching exercises before and after your practice sessions.

- **Playing With Feelings** - This is something that supersedes all other rules and something that you should focus on above everything else. A lot of times this will run in contrary with my two previous tips, but as you progress you'll slowly get the idea on how to play with feelings while being relaxed and economical in your movements.

For example, if a passage requires you to do aggressive strumming, don't be afraid to bring your hands way up and bring the pick down hard on the strings.

If you feel you need to pick or fret hard on a certain part of a song, go ahead. Just let your ears be your guide; you can do anything you want as long as you're getting the kind of sound that you want.

How To Sit Down And Hold The Guitar

Assuming that you are right handed and have a "normal" shaped guitar, you can just sit down on a comfortable chair and rest your guitar's body on your right leg like so

Fretting

In the most basic sense, fretting involves pressing down on the strings so that the fret wires are able to stop the strings at the correct pitch. Generally, you'd want your finger to land right in between the frets, whether playing a note or a chord. This often produces the best sound.

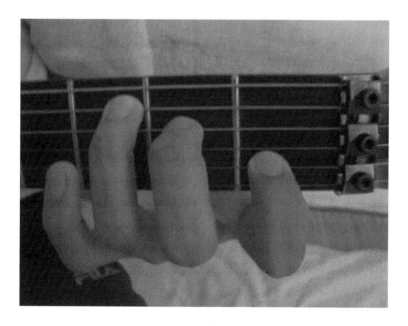

Fretting

- **Slide** - As the name suggests, this technique involves sliding up or down into a note. To do this, just pick the note first, then slide your fretting finger onto the fret of the next note.

- **Hammer-on's and Pull-off's** - To do a "hammer on", bring down your finger the fret but do not pick the string. A "pull off" usually comes after a hammer on because you can only pull off from a note that is already ringing out. A pull off involves releasing your fretting finger from the string with a slight flicking motion. Do not pick the string when you do this, the flicking motion will instead make the note ring out. Hammer-on's and pull-off's are typically done in quick successions.

Picking using a plectrum

Some beginner players usually make the mistake of focusing more on the fretting hand and not so much on the picking hand, only to discover later on that their fretting technique is pretty much rendered useless without the proper picking technique. This goes to show that the fretting hand and the picking hand need to develop TOGETHER. During your practice sessions, you'll need to do drills which will make your fretting hand move in perfect sync with your picking hand.

- **Holding the pick** - You'd want to hold the pick flat between the index finger and the thumb. Although you'll need to hold it tight enough so that it doesn't fall out, you'll need to loosen it up on occasion so that the pick won't come down too hard on the strings

How To Use The Downstroke, The Upstroke And, The Economy Picking

- **Downstroke** - The most basic stroke you'll use to pick the strings is the downstroke. As the name suggests, you'll need to use a downward motion to pick the strings.
- **Upstroke** - The opposite of the downstroke, you move the pick upward to pick the strings.
- **Economy Picking** - This is just a combination of downstrokes and upstrokes. Because the difference between a downstroke and an upstroke is barely noticeable during fast note runs, you can just use economy picking to shorten the time it takes for the tip of the pick to hit the strings. To do this, simply follow your downstroke with an upstroke, or the upstroke with a downstroke.

The Two Ways To "Attack" The Strings:

Flat

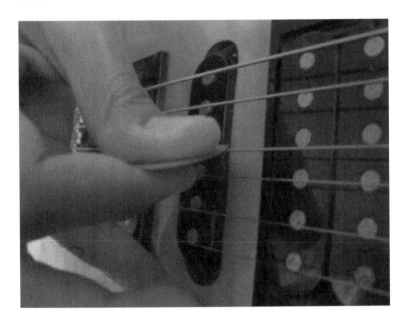

Bringing down the pick flat on the strings will make the note sharper and brighter. You'd want to do this to give emphasis to the note you wish to play, but your picking will slow down considerably since the pick will have to flex more and stay on the strings longer.

Angled

Playing with the pick at an angle will give you a "rounder" sound. Most players, especially those who use a lot of distortion prefect to keep their picks at an angle since the difference isn't that perceivable. You'll find that it can be easier to do quick succession of notes using economy picking with an angled pick.

Part 4 - Basic Chords and Scales

While it is totally possible to learn how to play the guitar without learning notation and music theory, you'll find out in the future that learning these will be INDISPENSABLE to your growth as a guitarist and a musician. However, since we will be focusing more on how you can make music on the guitar as soon as possible, an in depth discussion of music theory and notation is not yet needed.

Notes and Scales

Typically, you can get 47 notes out of a regular 22 fret necked guitar, although an electric guitar is a very flexible instrument and a lot of innovative players have shown that you can get more notes out of it.

If you know how to sing Do-Re-Mi, then you already know the Major Scale. Sing from La to La (la, ti, do, re, mi, fa, so, la) and you've got the Minor Scale. Now the starting point for these scales, Do for the Major Scale and La for the Minor Scale, can be any note of your choosing.

Now since the guitar is tuned to follow traditional Western Music, you'll be able to get all 7 notes of the Western Scale on it, including their "sharps" and "flats". You already know that the open strings are tuned to E, A, D, G, B, E, so here are the positions of the other notes:

Notes: E, F, G, A, B, C, D, E

I purposely left out the other notes for you to plot out, so you can better memorize the notes on the fretboard. However, here are some helpful hints if you are having a difficult time figuring it out:

- The notes on the E6 string and the E1 string are the same. (example: G can be found on the 3rd fret of the E6 string, as well as on the E1 string.)
- Any note should be the same and perfectly in tune with the note 5 frets behind it on the next string. (Example: E can be found on the 7th fret of the A5 string, as well as on the second fret of the D4 string). Except of course on the G string, any note on it should be the same as the note 4 frets behind it on the B string. (example: D can be found on the 7th fret on the G3 string, as well as on the 3rd fret of the B2 string.)

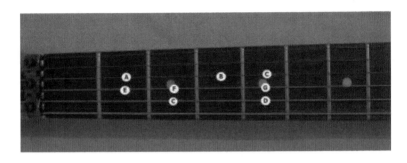

Notes from left to right: C, D, E, F, G, A, B, C

Why is it important to learn scales?

Most popular melodies that you know and hear are a play on scales. Scales take out a lot of guess work when learning melodies because it trains your ear to recognize notes relative to its position on the scale.

Demo: Star Spangled Banner

The Star Spangled Banner has a fairly recognizable melody. Try to pick out the notes from ear, so you can practice your picking technique and note recognition at the same time. If you cannot figure out some of the notes, try looking at the tab of the song below.

The tab for is a popular alternative to standard notation and is widely used on the Internet since it can be written in plain text. This format, however, is very lacking. Tab form can only tell you what notes to play, but does not tell you the duration of the note, the time signature etc.

Title: The Star-Spangled Banner

- Tempo = 120
- Electric Guitar
- Legend
- s - slide
- b – bend
- h - hammer on/pull off

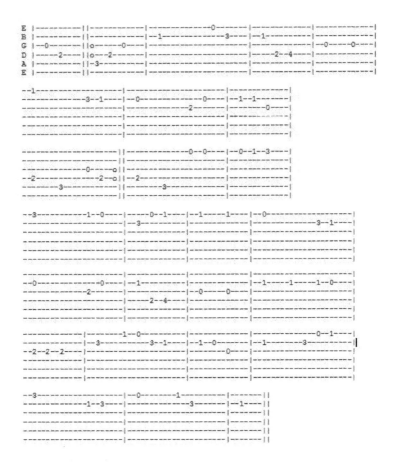

Chords

Chords are a bunch of notes struck together simultaneously. You may notice that you can create a mind-boggling number of chords, but for the sake of brevity I will show you how to play the most used forms of major and minor chords. These chords will allow you to play almost any popular song.

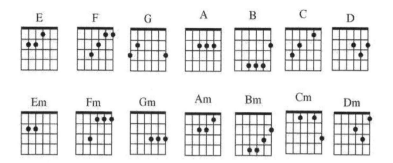

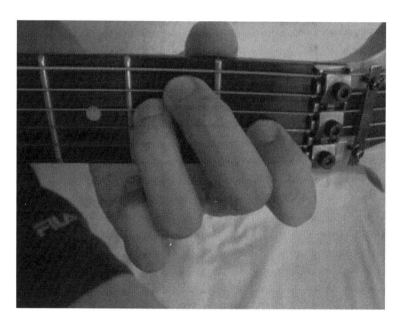

E (Major)

E Minor (Em)

F (Major)

F Minor (Fm)

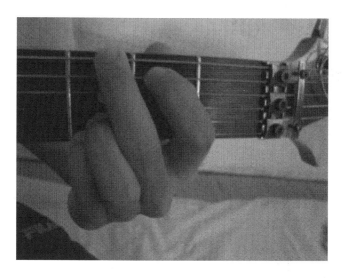

G (Major)

G Minor (Gm)

A (Major)

A Minor (Am)

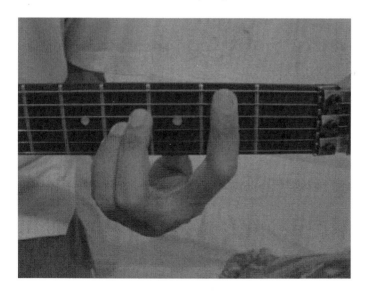

B (Major)

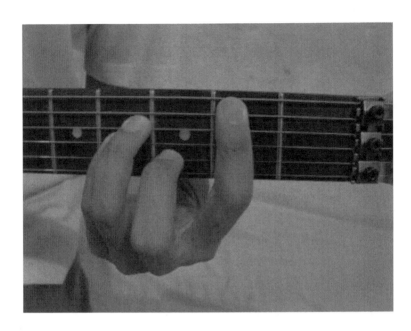

B Minor (Bm)

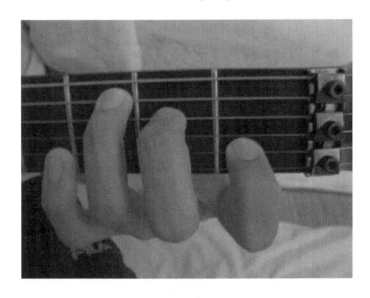

C (Major)

C Minor (Cm)

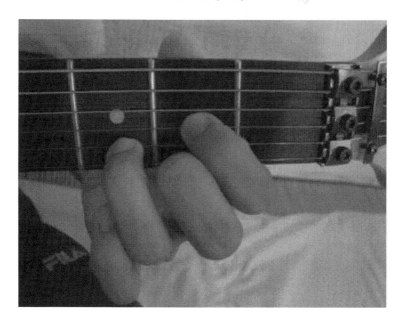

D (Major)

D Minor (Dm)

Of course you will encounter songs that use chords aside from the major and minor ones, so I'll include a chord chart at the end of this guide. You may find this useful especially if you like using song books.

Demo: John Denver - Leaving On A Jetplane

```
G                    C
```
1) All my bags are packed, I'm ready to go
2) There's so many times I've let you down
3) Now the time has come to leave you

```
    G                C
```
1) I'm standing here outside your door
2) So many times I've played around
3) One more time, let me kiss you

```
    G            C          D
```
1) I hate to wake you up to say goodbye
2) I tell you now, they don't mean a thing
3) Then close your eyes, I'll be on my way

```
         G              C
```
1) But the dawn is breakin' it's early morn
2) Every place I go, I'll think of you
3) Dream about the days to come

```
    G              C
```
1) The taxi's waitin' he's blowin' his horn
2) Every song I sing, I'll sing for you
3) When I won't have to leave alone

```
    G          C          D
```
1) Already I'm so lonesome I could die
2) When I come back I'll bring your wedding ring
3) About the times I won't have to say:

Chorus: (1, 2 & 3)
```
  G         C          G          C
```
So kiss me and smile for me; tell me that you'll wait for me
```
G           C        D
```
Hold me like you'll never let me go
```
       G     C
```
'Cause I'm leavin' on a jet plane
```
G          C         G
```
Don't know when I'll be back again
```
   C         D
```
Oh, babe, I hate to go....

Part 5 - Conclusion

Now that you already know a few things to help you figure out songs that you would like to play

Electric Guitar Maintenance Tips

How To Clean and Store Your Electric Guitar

Cleaning an electric guitar is pretty simple. All you'll need is a dry cloth to wipe the body and the neck. When cleaning the guitar's metal parts (strings, tuning head, strap pins), apply a bit of machine oil or WD-40 on the cloth then rub the metal parts with it. This will make your guitar look new.

An electric guitar, no matter how rugged its construction may be, is still a precision instrument which needs to be stored properly. Ideally, you should keep your instrument in a gig bag or a hard case, but if you do not have this, you can temporarily store your guitar somewhere dry with just the right temperature.

How To Change The Electric Guitar Strings

This should be a fairly easy task on a fixed bridged guitar, since you will just need to run the string through the body or the tailpiece (a kind of bridge that doesn't run the string through the body of the guitar).

New strings will need to stretch, so you'll need to tug on the strings right after putting them on your guitar. To stretch them properly, fret the string on the first fret, then tug on them near the bridge. Repeat this until you reach the very last fret. Do the same on all 6 strings.

Hand And Body Care Tips

Since you'll be playing mostly with a pick, it is a good idea to keep your nails short on both hands. You also would want to avoid doing anything that can strain your hands and fingers, or any activity that would expose your hands to sudden heat and cold.

Since you are a beginner, it is normal for your hands to get tired easily. If you're starting to feel pain in your hands, take a break. Shake your hands and arms to release tension. Don't forget to stretch your back and neck occasionally; this will also help you avoid pain.

Practice Tips

If you want to take your guitar playing to the next level and go beyond playing songs for yourself, you'll need to PRACTICE. It is the only way to get better at anything. Practice should be more than playing songs, and in case you're wondering how you should spend your practice time, here's a list of stuff you can try out:

1. Stretching and Warm ups - Since playing will require a lot of movement and difficult positions for your hands and fingers, you'll need to warm them up before going all out. Bend your fingers back a bit and then shake them to get the blood going.

Play a couple of runs of the Major Scale and Minor Scale, using a different note as your staring point on every run. This will help your ear get accustomed to the sound of the Major and Minor Scale, as well as help your fingers get warmed up. Play the scale slowly at first, then try to speed it up on the next run.

2. Practicing chords - There's only one way to do this, and that is to play and learn new songs! While each of us have their own favorite genre of music, I would recommend exploring contemporary pop and love songs as songs from this genre typically use very nice sounding chords and chord changes. This is a good way to get your hands accustomed to playing chords, memorize chord shapes and also expand your repertoire.

3. Learn melodies - Since you already have a basic idea on how scales work, you can now try and learn some well known melodies by ear, using scales as your guide. Sometimes all it takes is for you to get a note of a certain melody exactly right, and from there you can figure out the rest relative to this one note. Practicing this will help you get better at figuring out melodic lines faster, which will come in handy during improvised solos.

VI. Chord Chart

Key of C

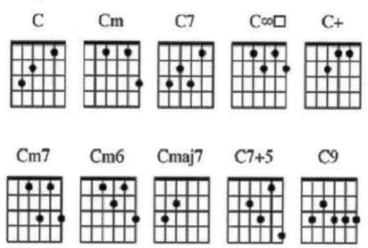

Key of C# or Db

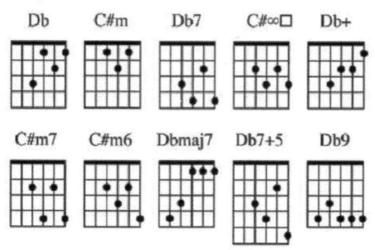

Key of D

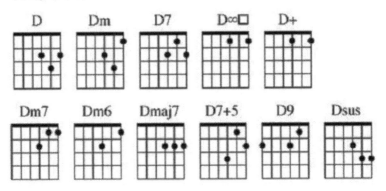

Key of D# or Eb

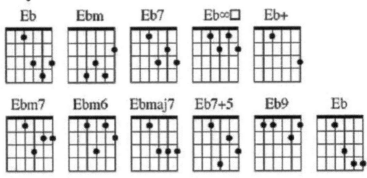

Key of E

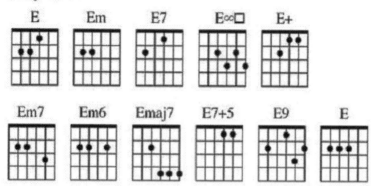

Key of F

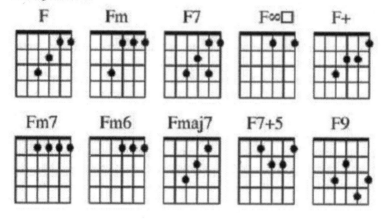

Key of F# or Gb

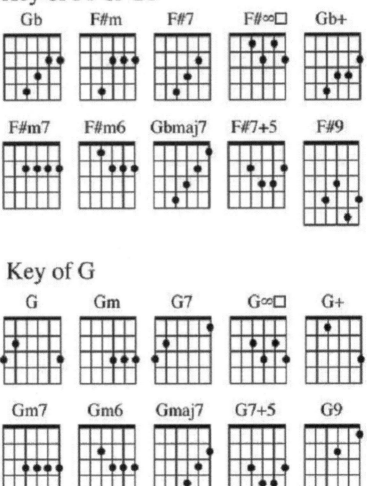

Key of G

Key of G# or Ab

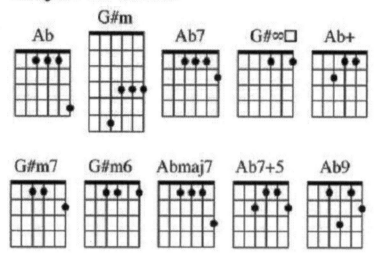

Key of A

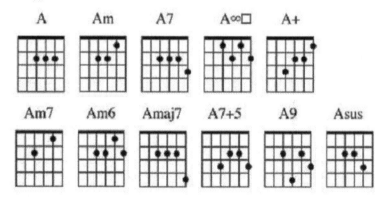

Key of A# or Bb

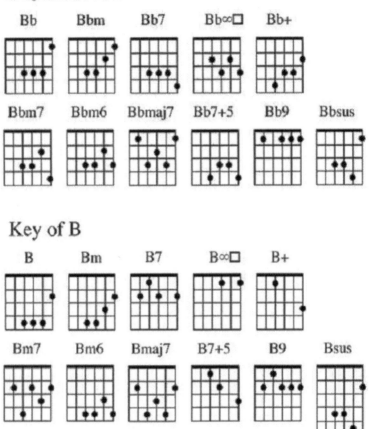

Recommended Resources

www.HowExpert.com – Quick 'How To' Guides on Unique Topics by Everyday Experts.

www.HowExpert.com/writers- Write About Your #1 Passion/Knowledge/Experience.

www.HowExpert.com/membership - Learn a New 'How To' Topic About Practically Everything Every Week.

www.HowExpert.com/jobs - Check Out HowExpert Jobs.

Made in the USA
Columbia, SC
06 December 2019